Mountain Star

Find a path that touches your heart;
follow that path to the end;
and may the beautiful stars
that grace the night sky
always bring you home safely.

*Dedicated in loving memory
to Charlie Fowler*

FOR ALL MOUNTAINEERS, STARGAZERS, CHILDREN and UNCLES ...

Copyright © 2008 by Mountain World Media, LLC

ISBN: 978-0-9763309-3-6

FIRST EDITION

Published by Mountain World Media LLC, Telluride, Colorado USA

Designed by Daiva Chesonis

IMAGE CREDITS
Backgrounds: ©iStockphoto.com/Selahattin Bayram, ©iStockphoto.com/Selahattin Bayram,
                    ©iStockphoto.com/Amanda Rohde
Earth: ©iStockphoto.com/Klaas Lingbeek van Kranen
Tripod: ©iStockphoto.com/A-Digit
Pencils: ©iStockphoto.com/Boris Yankov
Wood Floor: ©iStockphoto.com/Eric Vega
Child Silhouettes: ©iStockphoto.com/Simon Spoon
Bio Photos: ©Damon Johnston, ©Climbing

Visit our website at www.mountainworldmedia.com

Printed on recycled paper using soy inks

This is the true and heartfelt story
told through the eyes of a little girl,
who taught her friend to draw
a perfectly balanced star,
while also telling the story
of an adventurous climber.

Read this tender story and learn
how to draw your own perfect star!

Before you start, you might want to get
a piece of paper and a pencil or a crayon.

That way, you're ready to practice drawing stars!

Growing up, Lindsey always heard adventurous tales of her Uncle Charlie. Uncle Charlie was a climber who traveled the world, meeting new people and exploring mountains that most people never even dreamed of climbing.

Through his travels, Uncle Charlie always enjoyed learning about new customs, new foods, hearing lively music, and seeing new mountains.

Some of the mountains were snow capped, and others were hot and rocky, but always the mountains were beautiful and called out to him to come climbing.

When Uncle Charlie saw a photograph or heard about a mountain in a remote far-away country, he would think, "now that's a mountain that I should climb!"

He would study and learn about the mountain, the weather, the people, the language, and then he would plan his trip.

Once he had organized all of his climbing gear, food, and supplies, Uncle Charlie headed out with his friends. They would go for weeks and months at a time. Uncle Charlie would take lots of photographs.

When he returned from a long trip, he would share his stories and pictures with anyone who would listen.

As a little girl, Lindsey loved to hear his wonderful tales of travel and climbing. She looked wide eyed at the photographs of people in distant and remote places and dreamed that some day she would travel to these same places and experience the things that Uncle Charlie saw on his trips around the world.

Uncle Charlie's favorite place was on the other side
of the world—the beautiful land of Tibet.

It was one of his favorites because the
people were kind, gentle and welcomed
him with food and drinks of yak butter tea.

One night, Lindsey looked out her window and saw stars twinkling brightly against the dark sky. She knew in her heart that these were the same stars her Uncle Charlie saw when *he* looked up at the sky

Lindsey thought of the stars,
and she thought of her Uncle Charlie.

It was amazing to think that all over the world, people looked up
at many of the same stars in the night sky.

A few days later,
a friend asked Lindsey
to teach her how to draw a star.

Lindsey knew right away
how she would teach
her friend!

Lindsey said, "Before you start to draw a star ...

... think of my Uncle Charlie."

"First, Uncle Charlie goes UP the mountain."

"Then, Uncle Charlie comes DOWN the mountain."

"Next, Uncle Charlie goes to this side of the mountain."

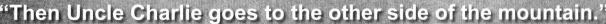

"Then Uncle Charlie goes to the other side of the mountain."

"And then Uncle Charlie comes home."
There, right before their eyes, was a perfectly balanced star!

Her friend could not believe it, and together she and Lindsey drew star after star after star. Some were big stars, and some were little stars.

That's because sometimes
Uncle Charlie climbed big mountains ...

and sometimes he climbed
little mountains.

Now YOU try it.

Trace your finger up the mountain,
down the mountain, to one side of the mountain,
to the other side of the mountain, and now back home.

Lindsey wants you to draw many perfect stars. Put them on your papers, hang them up in your room, and always think of her Uncle Charlie.

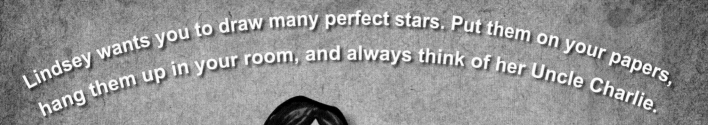

The End

Ginny Fowler Hicks

Ginny Fowler Hicks was born in North Carolina and grew up in Northern Virginia. She attended George Mason University and after graduation moved to Oregon where she currently lives with her husband Maurie. Ginny has been an elementary teacher and principal for the past 30 years and has read many children's books to students over the years. In 2001 Ginny was named Outstanding Women Educator by Alpha Delta Kappa and in 2006 she was the National Distinguished Principal from Oregon. "Mountain Star" is her first book and is written in memory of her brother Charlie Fowler.

Lindsey Hicks

As a young girl growing up in Oregon, Lindsey always looked forward to her Uncle Charlie's visits. He would set up the slide projector and show amazing photographs and tell engaging stories about his travels all around the world. She developed a love for travel and adventure by listening to her uncle's stories. Lindsey currently works as a certified child life specialist at a children's hospital in Phoenix, Arizona. She uses many children's books in her work. She helps to reduce the stress and anxiety that children and families experience during hospitalization. Lindsey promotes the importance of play and provides therapeutic and medical play opportunities every day in her work. She hopes this book inspires lots of drawing and travel.

Charlie Fowler

Charlie was born in North Carolina and grew up in Virginia, graduating from the University of Virginia with a degree in environmental science in 1975. He then moved to Colorado, finally settling on the Western Slope in the small town of Norwood and made a living through guiding, writing, photography and films. He successfully climbed the 8,000-meter peaks of Mount Everest, Cho Oyu, and Shishapangma. Between expeditions, he established hundreds of climbing routes at the small crags he founded throughout the desert Southwest. In recent years, he explored unnamed peaks in Tibet and remote areas of China. In recognition of his climbing accomplishments, he was awarded the 2004 Robert and Miriam Underhill Award for outstanding mountaineering achievement by the American Alpine Club. Active in his community, Charlie sat on the boards of the Telluride Mountain Club, the Horizon Program, and Mountainfilm in Telluride, and helped design and build several community climbing walls. With friend and climbing partner Damon Johnston, he founded Mountain World Media in 2005. Together they published several regional climbing guidebooks. On their list was to create a children's book that would capture the essence of mountaineering and the remote cultures encountered along the way. In October 2006, Charlie left for China with his climbing partner, Christine Boskoff, to attempt several unclimbed peaks. It was from this fifth trip to the region that Charlie did not come home. He and Chris died in an avalanche while attempting a new route on Mount Genyen. Although his pink mountaineering boots have been stilled, the bright legacy of a true "Mountain Star" shines on.

Anjali Sawant

Anjali was born in Coventry, England. She received her Bachelor of Fine Arts from California College of the Arts in 1981. Anjali now lives in the beautiful mountain town of Telluride, Colorado, one of the many places where Charlie liked to climb. She has many interests but her main love is working as an artist, illustrator, and cartoonist. Her work has been displayed in Los Angeles, Telluride, Montreal, and a few other cities in between.

Daiva Chesonis

Daiva was born in Baltimore, Maryland, some time during the '60s. Although she has a BA in Russian Studies and an MA in Diplomacy, she can't seem to shake the graphic design bug that has inhabited her self-taught soul since the '80s. As one of Charlie's many climbing partners, she has spent countless days wandering around the Southwest looking for that next "classic" route and dearly misses picking him up in Norwood on the way to the "wild, wild west" for another day of exploration. Daiva is working on *writing* a non-fiction book about walls and swears it will not be designed by her. Her other big project is Olivija (see below), a seven-year old for whom it all matters.

Olivija Berry

Truth be told, it was a handmade eight-page book that Olivija put together at preschool one afternoon that jump-started "Mountain Star." She had been taught how to draw a star by Ginny a few months earlier. When she proudly presented her creation "How to Make Stars" to her mom, Daiva, she said she had made it for her two-year-old cousin. It was realized right then that not only did the Mountain Star method work, but it was also a story worth sharing that will now be enjoyed by many.

SPECIAL THANKS TO
John McCall for his generous support;
Lise Waring and Lori Rozycki for editing advice; and
Allen Hill, John McCall, and the Christine Boskoff Collection
for additional photos of Charlie.